From Plowboy to Prophet

Being a Short History of Joseph Smith,
for Children

BY WILLIAM A. MORTON
(Illustrations by L. A. Ramsey)

British Library Cataloguing-in-Publication Data
A catalogue record for this book is available from the
British Library

Joseph Smith, the Prophet.

CONTENTS.

CONTENTS.

From Plowboy to Prophet.

BIRTH OF JOSEPH SMITH.

My dear little friends:—I am going to tell you a wonderful story. It is one of the most interesting stories you have ever heard. It is also one of the best, because it is all true, from beginning to end.

The story was told to me many years ago, and it made me feel happier than ever I felt before.

You have all heard the beautiful story of the birth of the dear Lord Jesus. That story, as you know, had its beginning in a lowly manger, in the little town of Bethlehem, not far from Jerusalem.

The story I am going to tell you had its beginning in a small, frame house, which once stood in the

2

little town of Sharon, Windsor County, Vermont. It was surrounded by a number of beautiful shade trees, and in it there lived a poor, but happy family by the name of Smith. The family consisted of Joseph Smith, the father, Lucy Smith, the mother, six sons and three daughters.

If you had lived in Sharon at the time of which I speak, and had taken a peep into that humble home on the 23rd of December--just two days before Christmas—1805, you would have seen a good, kind mother lying upon a soft, warm bed, and a little, new-born babe sleeping peacefully on her bosom. The woman was Mrs. Lucy Smith, and the child which nestled in her loving arms was the baby Joseph, God's precious Christmas gift to her, and also to the whole world.

Day after day friends and neighbors called to see Mrs. Smith and her baby. They took the little one gently in their arms and kissed his dear, sweet, innocent lips, but not one of them knew that they were looking upon the great Prophet of the last days.

At the proper time the baby was christened. He was given the name of Joseph Smith. That, you know, was also the name of his father.

LIGHT FROM THE SCRIPTURES.

The Smith family was poor. Their farm was not a very good one, and the father and mother had to work hard for the support of themselves and their children.

As soon as the girls were able to help in the home, and the boys on the farm, they willingly did so.

In the picture you see the boy Joseph ploughing with a yoke of oxen. He had very little time for school, but in the evenings, when his work was done, he studied at home, and learned to read and write, and to work simple examples in arithmetic. I am sure he often felt sorry that he was not able to go to school as much as the other boys. But, then, he must have felt happy in the thought that he was helping to lighten the burdens of his parents.

Joseph Assisting His Father on the Farm.

When Joseph was ten years of age his father left his place in Sharon and moved the family to Palmyra, in the State of New York. Four years later they left Palmyra and went to live in the town of Manchester, in the same State.

At that time the people in that part of the country became very much excited over religious matters. Almost every evening meetings were held in the churches. Joseph's mother and two of his brothers and a sister joined the Presbyterian Church. But Joseph did not unite himself with any church. I suppose you would like to know the reason why. Well, the reason was because they all taught different doctrines, and he did not know which one taught the true Gospel, or which was the true Church.

I think I know, to a certain extent, how he felt. One day I went to a railway depot in England to take a train for London. There were six or seven trains standing on different tracks, all waiting the signal to start. I did not know which train to take, and for a little while I stood puzzled. Just then I caught sight of a sign-board, on which was printed in large letters,

"Train for London on track 7."

Then I knew what to do. I boarded the train on the seventh track, and in due time arrived in London.

In the same way Joseph Smith was puzzled concerning the churches. How was he to know which of them was the true Church? Well, the Lord had prepared means, just as the railway company in England had prepared signs to direct people to the trains they wished to take. The way in which Joseph found the truth is told in the next chapter.

Joseph Reading the Bible.

JOSEPH'S FIRST PRAYER. THE ANSWER.

One evening Joseph took down the large, family Bible, and began to read its sacred pages. The Lord was guiding him at that time, but the boy did not know it. As he read, he came to the fifth verse of the first chapter of the Epistle of James, which reads as follows, "If any of you lack wisdom, let him ask of God, that giveth to all men liberally and unbraideth not, and it shall be given him."

This scripture caused Joseph to stop and think, as you will see by looking at the picture. It made a great impression upon his mind. It seemed to say to him, "You wish to know which of the churches is the true Church. Well, if you will ask God He will tell you."

Joseph decided to do that. But he did not tell

any member of the family what was in his heart. He closed the Bible, put it back in its place, and then went to his bed, little dreaming that the next day he would have news which in the course of time would startle the whole world.

He awoke early the next morning, arose and dressed himself. The rest of the family were fast asleep, so, slipping quietly out of the house, Joseph made his way to a small grove not far from his father's home. It was a beautiful spring morning. The sun was gilding the hill tops, the birds were singing their songs in the trees, and the air was scented with the fragrance of wild flowers. All nature seemed to say, "God lives. God is good. He loves His children and delights to bless them."

Selecting a suitable spot in the grove, Joseph knelt down and began to call upon God in earnest prayer. While he was praying he saw an exceedingly bright light coming down out of heaven. He gazed in astonishment on this strange sight, while a peace-

Joseph Praying in the Grove.

ful influence filled his soul. As the light reached the tops of the trees, Joseph beheld in the midst of it two heavenly Beings. They were in the form of men, but far more glorious and beautiful. They were God the Father and Jesus Christ His Son. Pointing to the Son, the Father said, "Joseph, this is my beloved Son, hear Him."

As soon as Joseph was able to speak he asked the Lord which of the churches was the true Church. He was surprised when the Lord told him that all the churches had departed from the right way, that they had been established by men and not by God, that none of them taught the true Gospel, and that he was not to join any of them.

Then the Lord told Joseph that in due time the true Church would be set up again on earth, and that if he were true and faithful he would be chosen to be its leader and Prophet.

Filled with wonder and surprise, Joseph arose and returned to his home.

HOW JOSEPH'S STORY WAS RECEIVED.

Joseph felt very strange all the rest of the day. He could think of nothing but the wonderful vision he had had, and the things which the Lord had told him. But these things had not been revealed to him just for his own benefit. Others should know of them as well as he. Yes, he would tell the people the glad tidings, so that they might rejoice with him, and look forward with joy to the time when the true Church would be again established in the earth.

Who should he tell first? Why, who but one of the ministers, and he in turn could tell all the members of his church. So, with a glad heart, Joseph went to the minister of one of the churches and told him about the glorious vision he had had in the grove, and also the things which the Lord had told him.

You can imagine how the boy felt when the minister turned to him and said, "I do not believe one word of what you have told me. It is all of the wicked one. There are no such things as visions and revelations in these days." But Joseph knew better. He knew that he had had a vision. He knew that he had seen the Father and the Son, and that the Lord had talked with him. People might mock his testimony and refuse to believe it, but that would not rob him of the knowledge he had received from God.

In a short time the news concerning Joseph's vision reached the ears of the ministers of the different churches in the neighborhood. What effect did it have upon them? I am sorry to tell you that it had much the same effect that the telling of Joseph's dreams had upon his brethern, that the news of the Savior's birth had upon Herod, and the testimony of Stephen had upon the people who heard it— it made them very angry, and aroused in their hearts a deadly hatred against him.

At that time Joseph was only a boy. His tender

age alone ought to have protected him, but it did not. He was treated as if he were a full-grown man, and also as one of the greatest impostors the world had ever seen.

The courage which the boy displayed was truly marvelous. From every quarter he received bitter persecution, but as the Prophet Daniel stood undaunted in the midst of the lions, so Joseph Smith stood in the midst of his enemies. He never flinched from his position. Who gave him such courage? Who enabled him to stand alone? Who gave courage to Joseph, the son of Jacob, to defend the truth which had been revealed to him? Who gave courage to David to enable him to fight the giant Goliath? Who gave courage to Daniel to enter the den of lions? Who gave courage to the three Hebrews to face the fiery furnace? Who gave courage to Stephen to die for the truth? It was the God of Heaven. It was He, also, who sustained the boy Joseph Smith in the midst of all his trials and persecutions.

JOSEPH VISITED BY THE ANGEL MORONI.

I am now going to tell you about another wonderful thing. It took place one night in September, three years from the time Joseph had seen the glorious vision in the grove.

Joseph had just gone to bed. As he lay there his thoughts wandered back to the morning when, in answer to prayer, the Father and Son had appeared to him. He felt that he would like to know if the Lord was still pleased with him. He began to pray, believing firmly that his prayer would be answered. And so it was.

While Joseph was praying, a bright, heavenly light entered the room. The light increased, and in a few minutes the little bed-chamber was filled with it. On looking up, Joseph was greatly startled.

Close beside his bed stood a heavenly messenger, his feet a short distance from the floor. This holy being was the Angel Moroni. He had come with a very important message from the Lord.

The angel was clothed in a robe of spotless white. His head, hands and feet were bare. His face was as bright as the sun at noonday. He called Joseph by name, and then began to tell him about a great work which the Lord had marked out for him.

Joseph listened with the greatest interest while the angel talked to him. He told him about a wonderful record, or history, which had been hidden from the world for hundreds of years. It was written in a strange language, upon gold plates, and was buried in the Hill Cumorah, not far from Joseph's home. It was a history of the people who lived in this land long before and after the time of the Savior.

It also told about Jesus appearing to them, after

Visit of the Angel Moroni.

His resurrection, and of the glorious gospel which
He had taught them.

The angel said that in the course of time the
Lord would permit Joseph to take the plates from
their hiding place. He would also help him to translate the writing upon them into the English language.
After that the book would go into all the world, and
the people would learn of the wonderful things which
the Lord had done among the early inhabitants of
this land.

Moroni told Joseph many other important
things. When he had delivered his message, the
angel departed.

As Joseph lay thinking over what had taken
place, the light again entered his room. Then the
angel appeared the second time, and repeated all
that he had said before, adding some things. He
then took his departure, but in a short time re-ap-
peared, and delivered the same message. He told
Joseph that when he received the plates he would

have to take great care of them, and hold them as a sacred gift from God.

The vision closed, and the angel disappeared.

JOSEPH VISITS CUMORAH AND VIEWS THE PLATES.

Joseph's interview with the angel lasted the whole night. When the morning came he arose and attended to his chores as usual. He did not tell anyone what had happened during the night.

After breakfast, he went with his father to the field, but he was so weak that he could not work. His father, seeing that he was not feeling well, told him to go home.

Joseph started for the house, but in trying to climb a fence his strength failed him, and he fell helpless to the ground. He lay unconscious for some time. When he recovered he looked up and saw the Angel Moroni.

The heavenly messenger repeated what he had told

him the previous night. He then told Joseph to go back to his father and tell him all that had taken place.

Mr. Smith listened to his son's story with interest and astonishment. It was, indeed, a wonderful thing. But he knew that Joseph had told the truth, for he was a good, honest, truthful boy. Indeed, Joseph could not have told such a story if it had not been true. What boy ever thought of such things? Not one in all the world.

Joseph's father told him that what he had seen and heard was of God, and that he must do all that the angel told him. By this time Joseph felt better, and he started for the Hill Cumorah.

On arriving at the hill, he went straight to the place where the plates were buried. It had been shown to him in vision the night before. He saw a stone just a little above the ground. With the aid of a lever he raised it, and there, in a box made of four flat stones, lay the gold plates.

Joseph Visits Cumorah and Views the Plates.

Beside the plates was a curious instrument, called the Urim and Thummim. It was like a pair of large spectacles. It had been put there to aid Joseph in translating the writing upon the plates.

Joseph put forth his hands to take the plates from their hiding place. At that moment the Angel Moroni appeared and stopped him. He said the time had not come for Joseph to get the sacred history. He told Joseph to come to the hill on the same day each year for four years. At the end of that time, if he should prove faithful, the Lord would let him take the plates.

Joseph put the stone lid back on the box, covered it over as before, and returned to his home to begin the work of preparing himself for his great mission.

JOSEPH RECEIVES THE PLATES.

During the next two years Joseph helped his father on the farm. He also worked for neighboring farmers. He did his work well, and his employers were pleased with him.

Then he went to work in an old silver mine. It was owned by a man named Josiah Stoal. At the end of a month Joseph got Mr. Stoal to stop working the mine, as there was no sign that it would pay. But Mr. Stoal did not want to part with Joseph, so he kept him to do other work.

While working for this man, Joseph boarded with a family by the name of Hale. Mr. Hale had a daughter named Emma. Joseph and Emma grew to love each other, and in the course of time they were married. After his marriage, Joseph went to work again for his father.

Finally the time came for Joseph to get the plates. It was the 22nd of September, 1827. With feelings of joy and fear Joseph started for Cumorah. At the hill he was met by the Angel Moroni. The cover was taken off the stone box, the sacred record was lifted from its hiding place and placed in the hands of Joseph.

The heavenly messenger then told him to take the greatest care of the plates, and not to let them pass out of his hands. The plates were about eight inches long, and each one was almost as thick as common tin. They were bound together with three rings. They made a book about six inches thick. Part of the record was sealed. The angel told Joseph that when he had translated the unsealed part he would come and take charge of the plates again.

When it became known that Joseph had the plates, wicked men did all in their power to get them. But they did not succeed, for Joseph remembered the instruction of the angel, and kept them hid.

Persecution became so strong in Manchester that Joseph and his wife decided to go to Pennsylvania, to the home of Mr. Hale, Emma's father. But how to get there they did not know. It was nearly one hundred and fifty miles, and Joseph had no money.

But the Lord sent help to His servant. He put it into the heart of a man named Martin Harris to give Joseph fifty dollars to help him on his journey. Joseph felt very grateful for this kindness, and from that time Martin Harris became one of his best friends.

With his wife and the sacred record Joseph started in a wagon for Pennsylvania. One day wicked men stopped him. They searched the wagon for the plates but failed to find them. Joseph had hidden them in a barrel of beans.

At the home of Mr. Hale, Joseph began to copy the characters which were upon the plates, and to translate them into the English language.

Copy of Characters on the Plates.

PROFESSOR ANTHON'S TESTIMONY.

Joseph spent about two months copying and translating the characters which were upon the plates. Some of the characters are shown on the opposite page. That kind of writing looks very strange to us. How hard it would be for a person to translate this writing into English. Joseph could not have done such a thing without the help of the Lord.

One day Martin Harris went to Mr. Hale's home to visit the Prophet. He asked Joseph if he would let him take some of the characters he had copied and translated, to New York, to show to a learned man there.

Joseph said he could do so. On arriving in New York, Mr. Harris went to Professor Charles Anthon. This man was able to speak several languages. Mr.

Harris showed him the work Joseph had done, and asked him to give his opinion about it.

Professor Anthon looked at the characters which Joseph had copied, also the translation. He said the characters were true, and that the translation was correct. He gave Mr. Harris a letter to this effect.

Just as Mr. Harris was about to leave, Professor Anthon said to him, "How did the young man find out that there were gold plates in the place where he found them?" Mr. Harris said an angel of God had revealed it to him.

On hearing that, the professor said, "Let me see that letter." Mr. Harris took it out of his pocket and handed it to him. The learned man tore it into pieces, saying there were no such things now as the ministering of angels.

Professor Anthon told Martin Harris that if he would bring the record to him he would translate it. Mr. Harris said he could not do so, as Joseph would not let anyone take the plates. He also told the professor that part of the plates was sealed. On hearing that, the learned man said, "I cannot read a sealed book." Martin Harris went back to Joseph and told him all that Professor Anthon had said.

I am now going to show you how a prophecy was fulfilled at that time. You have all heard of the Prophet Isaiah. He lived before the time of the Savior. He wrote a book; it is one of the books of the Bible. If you will turn to the twenty-ninth chapter of the book of Isaiah, you will find these words, beginning at the 11th verse:

"And the vision of all is become unto you as the words of a book that is sealed, which men deliver to one that is learned, saying, Read this, I pray thee: and he saith, I cannot; for it is sealed."

That prophecy was fulfilled when Martin Harris took the copy of the characters and the translation to Professor Anthon. When told that a part of the record was sealed, the learned man said, "I cannot read a sealed book."

The book was given to Joseph Smith, who was no[t] learned, and he, by the gift and power of God, trans[s]lated it into the English language. That preciou[s] record is the Book of Mormon.

WHAT HAPPENED THROUGH THE BREAKING OF A PROMISE.

Martin Harris was greatly interested in the Prophet Joseph and in the work which he was doing. Soon after his visit to Professor Anthon, he went to Joseph and told him he would like to write for him while he translated the engravings upon the plates. Joseph accepted this kind offer and Mr. Harris became his scribe.

The work of translation was very slow and also very difficult. But it gave Joseph and Martin great joy. They were in the service of the Lord. What a wonderful history they were preparing! Tens of thousands of people would rejoice when they read of the great things which the Lord had done among the early inhabitants of this land.

At the end of two months Martin Marris had written 116 large pages of the translation. His wife had asked him a number of times for permission to see what he had written.

One day Martin asked Joseph to let him take the papers away, to show to a few friends. Joseph refused to do so. Then Martin wanted Joseph to ask the Lord about the matter. The Prophet did so, and received an answer, through the Urim and Thummim, telling him not to let Martin have the papers.

But Martin was not satisfied. He asked Joseph to enquire of the Lord again. The answer was the same as before. A third time Martin asked for the same thing. Then the word of the Lord came to Joseph saying he might allow Martin Harris to take the papers, but that he, Joseph, would be held responsible for them.

Martin promised Joseph that he would let only five persons see the papers. These were his wife, his father and mother, his brother, and his wife's sister. I am sorry to say that Martin Harris failed to keep his promise. He let wicked men have the sacred writings. They kept them, and neither Martin nor Joseph ever saw them again. ,

Joseph was punished for doing as Martin asked him. The Urim and Thummim was taken from him, so that he could not translate. The Prophet had great sorrow because of this. He humbled himself before the Lord and prayed for forgiveness. At length his prayer was answered, his sin was pardoned, and the Urim and Thummim given back to him.

Martin Harris was more severely punished. He lost his place as scribe, and was never allowed to write again for the Prophet. What a serious thing it is for a person to break a promise made to the Lord, or even to one of His servants!

THE AARONIC PRIESTHOOD RESTORED.

Joseph felt sorry at losing the help of Martin Harris. He had now no one to write for him. He prayed to the Lord to send some one to assist him. His prayer was answered; the help came.

One Sabbath evening a young man named Oliver Cowdery called at the home of Mr. Hale, and enquired for Joseph. He was introduced to the Prophet. He told Joseph he had just come from Manchester, where he had been teaching school. He had heard that Joseph had been visited by heavenly Beings, and had prayed to the Lord to know if the report were true. He received a testimony that Joseph had been called of God to do a great work, and was also told that he had been chosen to assist the Prophet.

Oliver said he would be glad to write for Joseph.

hn the Baptist Conferring the Aaronic Priesthood on Joseph Smith and Oliver Cowdery.

His offer was accepted, and two days later Joseph again began the work of translating, Oliver writing for him.

One day in May, 1829, they came to a passage in the sacred record which caused them to stop and think seriously. It spoke of baptism for the remission of sins. Joseph and Oliver had not been baptized. What were they to do?

After talking the matter over for some time, they decided to pray to the Lord about it. They went to the woods, and there they asked the Lord to make plain to them the meaning of baptism for the remission of sins.

In answer to their prayer, a heavenly messenger appeared before them. He told them he was John the Baptist, the same who had baptized the Savior, and that he had been sent by the Apostles Peter, James and John to them. Placing his hands upon the heads of Joseph and Oliver, he uttered these words:

"Upon you my fellow servants, in the name of Messiah, I confer the Priesthood of Aaron, which holds the keys of the ministering of angels, and of the gospel of repentance and of baptism by immersion for the remission of sins; and this shall never be taken again from the earth until the sons of Levi do offer again an offering unto the Lord in righteousness."

He then told Joseph and Oliver to go down to the water and baptize each other. After giving them other instructions, he was taken up in the midst of a pillar of light.

Joseph and Oliver then went to the river and were baptized. Joseph baptized Oliver and then Oliver baptized Joseph. The power of God rested upon them, and by the gift of prophecy Joseph foretold of the establishment of the Church of Christ upon the earth in these last days.

With hearts filled with thanksgiving and gladness they returned to their work of translation.

The First Pastime. The Prophet Insult Pastime. Oliver Grayham

THE GOLD PLATES ARE SHOWN TO THREE WITNESSES.

At this time two of Joseph's brothers, Samuel H. and Hyrum, came to visit him. He was very glad to see them. He talked with them a long time. He told them about the visit of John the Baptist. This heavenly messenger had given him and Oliver Cowdery authority to baptize people for the remission of their sins. He and Oliver had been baptized.

Joseph told his brothers to pray to the Lord about this matter. They did so. The Lord gave them a testimony that what Joseph had told them was true. Then Joseph's brothers were baptized.

Joseph was very poor at that time. He had no money to buy food for his family. He was thinking about going out to work. Just then help was sent

4

him. A kind-hearted man named Joseph Knight, who lived in New York, had heard of the Prophet. He came to see him, and brought him a supply of food.

Soon after that, Joseph was visited by a young man named David Whitmer. He came with a message from his father, Peter Whitmer. Mr. Whitmer lived in Fayette, Seneca county, New York. He also had heard of the Prophet, and of the wonderful book he was translating. He invited Joseph and Oliver to come to his home and do the work there. He would keep them, free of charge, and would see that no harm came to them.

Joseph felt thankful for this kind offer. He said he would go. He and Oliver got ready to move to Fayette. But Joseph was troubled about the gold plates. He might be robbed of them on the way. Just then the Angel Moroni appeared and told Joseph that he would take charge of the plates.

After Joseph had been at Mr. Whitmer's home a short time he went out into the garden. He there met the Angel Moroni and received from him the sacred record.

The Whitmer family were very kind to Joseph and Oliver. They told some of their neighbors about the Prophet, and invited them to come and see him. Joseph told them about the great things which the Lord had done. Some of them believed his words and were baptized.

One day the Lord made known to Joseph that three witnesses were to see the gold plates. These men were Oliver Cowdery, David Whitmer, and Martin Harris. They felt very happy when they heard the news.

Joseph went to the woods with these three brethren. They all prayed to the Lord. But their prayer was not answered. They prayed again. Still no answer came. Then Martin Harris said he was the cause of their prayers not being answered. The Lord was not well pleased with him, because he had broken his promise to Joseph.

Martin Harris left the brethren. He felt very sorry. He went off by himself, to ask the Lord to forgive him. After he had gone, Joseph, Oliver and David began to pray. While they were doing so a bright light shone down upon them. Then the Angel Moroni appeared before them. He had with him the gold plates, also the Urim and Thummim.

The heavenly messenger turned over, one by one, the leaves of the part that was not sealed. The brethren saw the characters which were upon them. While they were looking upon the plates they heard a voice from heaven. It was the voice of the Lord. He said the record was true, and that it had been translated correctly. They were told to bear testimony to the world of the things they had seen and heard.

Then Joseph went to Martin Harris and they prayed together. Their prayer was answered. The angel came and showed the plates to Martin. He also heard the voice from heaven. He fell on his

The Angel Moroni Showing the Plates of the Book of Mormon to the Witnesses.

face, crying, "It is enough! Mine eyes have beheld! Mine eyes have beheld!"

The three witnesses then returned with the Prophet to the home of Peter Whitmer. You can find their testimony, also the testimony of eight other witnesses, in the front of the Book of Mormon.

THE MELCHIZEDEK PRIESTHOOD
RESTORED.

At last the work of translating was done. Then the Angel Moroni called for the plates. He still has charge of them. Part of them, you know, was sealed. Some time the sealed part will be translated. Then we will learn more about the great things which the Lord has done.

The book was now ready to be printed. Mr. Grandin, a printer in New York, said he would print and bind five thousand copies for three thousand dollars. He was given the work. Martin Harris gave security for the payment of the printing.

Then Joseph went back to Pennsylvania to visit his wife Emma. He told her how the Lord had blessed him in his work. It made her feel very happy.

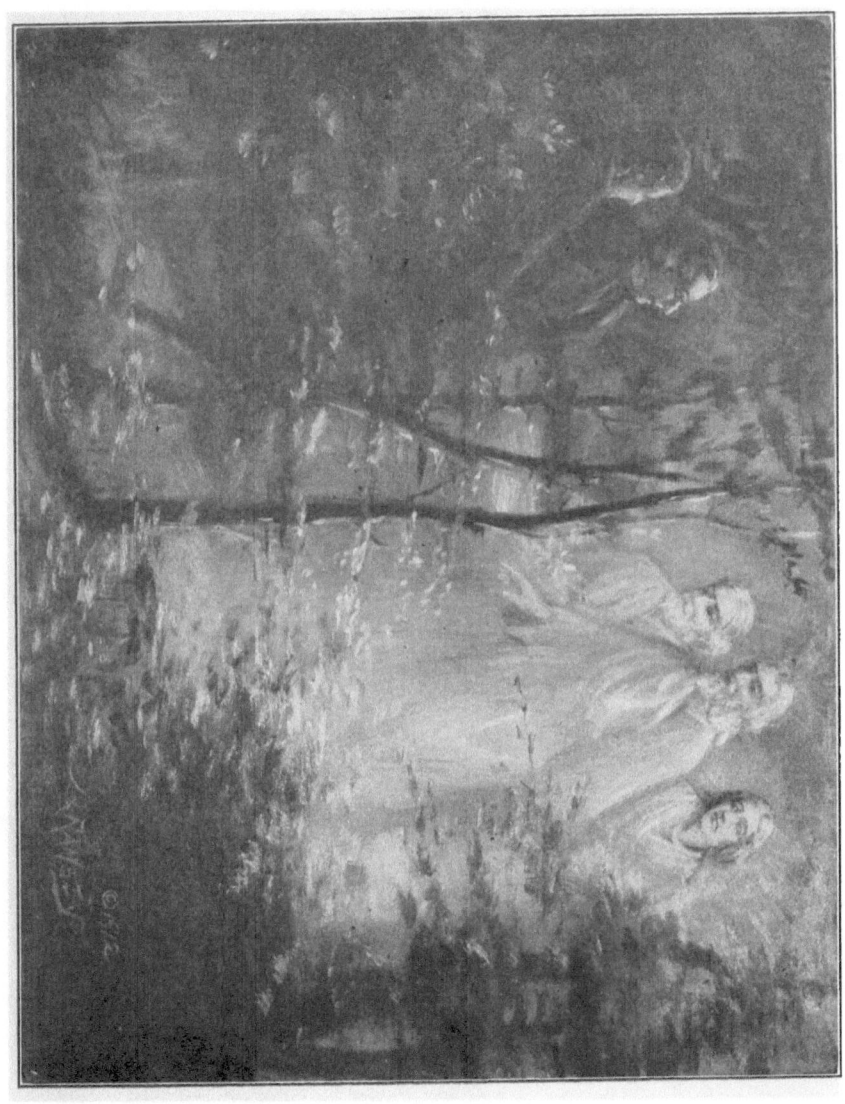

Visit of the Apostles Peter, James and John

Soon after that another wonderful thing took place. One day in June, 1829, Joseph and Oliver were in the State of New York. They were out in a quiet part of the country. They were talking about the Lord and about the great work He was helping them to do.

Just then three angels came down and stood before them. These heavenly visitors were three of the Lord's apostles. They were Peter, James and John. They told Joseph and Oliver that they had come to confer upon them the Melchizedek Priesthood. That would give them authority to lay on hands for the gift of the Holy Ghost. They could also organize the true Church of Christ again on the earth.

Then Peter, James and John placed their hands upon Joseph's head and ordained him the first Elder in the Church. They then ordained Oliver the second Elder.

In the year 1830, the Book of Mormon was published. On the 6th day of April, in the same year, a meeting was held at the house of Peter Whitmer. A number of people were present who had been baptized. Joseph asked them if they would like him and Oliver to be their leaders and teachers. They all said they would. The Sacrament was administered. Joseph and Oliver then laid their hands upon the heads of those who had been baptized, and confirmed them. On that day the Church of Jesus Christ of Latter-day Saints was organized.

THE FIRST MIRACLE.

The next Sunday after the Church was organized a meeting was held at the home of Peter Whitmer, senior. There were many people present. Oliver Cowdery preached to them. He told them about the Book of Mormon. He also told them about the visit of John the Baptist. He said if they would be baptized the Lord would forgive all their sins. Then they could be confirmed members of the true Church.

At the close of the meeting three men and three women were baptized in Seneca Lake. The following Sunday seven others were baptized.

At this time Joseph went to visit Mr. Knight. This man had been kind to the Prophet. He brought him a supply of food when he was translating the plates. The Knight family were glad to see Joseph. He stayed with them several days. Joseph held meetings in Colesville, where the Knight family lived.

Mr. Knight had a son named Newel. He talked with the Prophet often about the great latter-day work. He also attended the meetings. Joseph asked him several times to pray. He said he could not do so. One day he told Joseph he would pray at the next meeting. He did not keep his promise.

The next morning Newel went into the woods. He knelt down and tried to pray. But he was not able to speak. The Lord was not pleased with him. A strange feeling came over him.

He went back to his home feeling very bad and acted in a strange way. An evil spirit had entered into him. He suffered great pain. A number of relatives and friends heard what had taken place. They came to see him, but could not help him.

Mr. Knight told his wife to go for the Prophet. Joseph came quickly. He felt very sorry when he saw Newel. Joseph took hold of his hand. "There is an evil spirit in me, Joseph," said Mr. Knight, "and I want you to cast him out. I know you can do so."

Then the power of God was with the Prophet. He said to the evil spirit, "In the name of Jesus Christ I command you to come out of him."

At that moment the evil spirit left Mr. Knight. Newel was so weak that he had to be placed upon his bed. Then the Spirit of the Lord entered into him, and in a short time he was well again. He thanked and praised the Lord for healing him. He soon after joined the Church.

This was the first miracle wrought in the Church. Many who saw it believed it was done by the power of God. They also were baptized and became members of the Church.

HOW JOSEPH WAS SAVED FROM HIS ENEMIES.

On the 9th day of June, 1830, the first conference of the Church was held. There were thirty members present, also many others. The Sacrament was administered. Then some people who had been baptized were confirmed members of the Church.

That was a happy day for the Saints. The Holy Spirit was poured out upon them. Some prophesied, and others were given glorious visions.

Newel Knight was greatly blessed of the Lord. He saw, in vision, the Savior, seated beside His Father on a throne in the heavens. Mr. Knight was told the time would come when he would be with the Lord. Soon after the conference David Whitmer baptized a number of persons.

There were several people in Colesville who wanted to be baptized. Joseph and some of his brethren went there. Saturday afternoon they built a dam across a stream of water. They were going to baptize there the next day. But they were not able to do so, for during the night a mob gathered and tore down the dam.

The next day, the Sabbath, a meeting was held in the home of Mr. Knight. Some of the men who had broken the dam were there. They were pleased with what they had done. But Joseph and his brethren had a good plan in their minds. They arose early the next morning, re-built the dam, and baptized thirteen persons. One of them was Emma Smith, the Prophet's wife.

That made the mob very angry. They went to a police officer and told him things about Joseph which were not true. A meeting was to be held that evening. Before it took place the officer came and arrested Joseph. He told the Prophet a mob was waiting for him, but that he would be his friend, and save him, if he could.

Joseph and the officer got into a wagon. They had not gone far when the mob rushed out upon them. The wicked men thought the officer would turn Joseph over to them, but instead of doing that he drove quickly past them.

That angered them more. They ran as fast as they could after the wagon. Joseph and the officer were getting ahead, when suddenly one of the wheels came off. The two men jumped out of the wagon. They lifted the wheel, put it back in its place and fastened it. Then they sprang to their seats, put the whip to the horse, and were soon out of reach of the mob.

They drove to South Bainbridge. The officer engaged a room in a small hotel. He was afraid the mob might come during the night. So he made Joseph lie on the bed while he slept on the floor, with his feet against the door. He kept his loaded gun by his side. They were not disturbed.

The next day Joseph was tried in court. Two able men defended him. They proved to the judge that Joseph had not done any harm, and the Prophet was set free.

JOSEPH OPPOSED BY HIS BRETHREN.

The Lord had given Joseph a number of revelations. He and his wife Emma had written them. While reading one of these revelations, Oliver Cowdery thought he saw a mistake. He wrote at once to the Prophet, telling him to change certain words.

Joseph felt very sorry when he read the letter. He knew that what he had written was true. It had come from the Lord, and he would not change it.

A few days later Joseph went from Harmony to Fayette, to see Oliver Cowdery. Oliver was staying with the Whitmer family. He had led the Whitmers to believe that Joseph had made a mistake. They did not feel as kindly toward the Prophet as before. Joseph tried to reason with them, but they would not listen to him.

The Prophet prayed to the Lord to help him. Soon after that Oliver Cowdery and the Whitmers saw that they were wrong. They felt sorry for what they had done, and asked Joseph to forgive them, which he did. Then Joseph went back to Harmony, to the home of his father-in-law, Mr. Hale.

What a change he found there! While he had been at Fayette a wicked minister had visited the Hale family. He told them evil things about the Prophet. His stories were false, but the Hales believed them. From that time Mr. Hale and his family turned against Joseph, and opposed him and his work.

At this time Newel Knight and his wife came to visit the Prophet. It was decided to hold a meeting. Joseph went out to buy wine for the Sacrament. On the way he was stopped by a heavenly messenger. The angel told him not to buy any more wine from his enemies. The Saints were to make their own wine. If they could not do that, then water would be just as acceptable to the Lord. This explains the reason why we use water instead of wine in the Sacrament.

Joseph returned to the house. A little pure wine was made. Then a meeting was held and the Sacrament administered. There were only five persons present, but the Lord blessed them, and they had a happy time together. At that meeting Emma Smith and Mrs. Knight were confirmed members of the Church.

Soon after that, Joseph, his brother, Hyrum, John and David Whitmer set out to visit the Church at Colesville. There were many wicked men in that place. It was there that Joseph had been chased by a mob.

The Prophet and his brethren prayed to the Lord to take care of them, and He did. On the way to Colesville, Joseph and his companions passed a large number of men working on the road. Several of them were bitter enemies of the Prophet. They were looking out for him. But the Lord caused something to come over their eyes, so that when Joseph came up to them they did not know him.

The brethren reached Colesville in safety. A meeting was held at the home of Mr. Knight. A number of persons who had been baptized were confirmed. The members of the Church partook of the Sacrament. Then they all listened with delight while the Prophet and others preached to them.

The next day the mob heard that Joseph was at the home of Mr. Knight. They rushed to the place and demanded that the Prophet and his companions be turned out. Mr. Knight told them they had come too late, that Joseph and his brethren had left for Harmony several hours before.

In that time of trouble Joseph found a friend in Peter Whitmer. This good man invited the Prophet and his family to come and make their home with him in Fayette, and they did so.

There was a member of the Church at Fayette

named Hyrum Page. He was leading some of the Saints astray. He had a strange stone, by which he received revelations. But they had not come from the Lord. They were given by the evil one.

Joseph talked and prayed with the brethren. They saw that the revelations which Hyrum Page had received were not true. At that time the Lord gave a revelation to Oliver Cowdery through the Prophet Joseph Smith. He told Oliver that no one had been appointed to receive revelations for the Church except Joseph the Prophet. That settled the matter, and peace was restored.

Before closing this chapter, I wish to say to my young readers: There is only one man on the earth at a time appointed to receive revelations for the Church. That man is the President of the Church.

MISSION TO THE LAMANITES.

While the Prophet Joseph and Oliver Cowdery were translating the Book of Mormon they found many things which gave them great joy. Among them were glorious promises made by the Lord to the Lamanites, or Indians. The Book of Mormon would be taken to them. It would tell them where they came from, and the great things which the Lord had done for their forefathers. They would also learn the Gospel, and in the course of time many of their race would become white.

Joseph enquired of the Lord about these things. He was told that the time was near at hand when the Lamanites would also have the Gospel preached to them. The Lord was preparing men for that mission.

One of these was a man named Parley P. Pratt.

He and his wife lived in a little home in the wilderness, near Cleveland, Ohio. They were good people. Some time before, a young preacher named Sidney Rigdon had visited them. Mr. Pratt became a member of his church. Then he decided to give up farming and become a preacher. He sold all his goods, and started with his wife for New York, to visit relatives there. On reaching Newark, Mr. Pratt felt impressed to stop there, but Mrs. Pratt continued her journey. Why he should stop, he could not tell. He soon learned the reason.

At Newark, Parley P. Pratt first heard of the Prophet Joseph Smith and the Book of Mormon. He wondered if what he had heard of them was true. He would try to find out for himself.

For this purpose he went to the home of the Smith family, near Manchester, New York. There he learned from Hyrum Smith the truth about the whole matter. His heart was filled with joy as he listened to the glad tidings.

He and Hyrum then went to Fayette, where Mr. Pratt was introduced to Oliver Cowdery. He told Oliver he believed that Joseph Smith was a Prophet of God, and that the Book of Mormon was a true record. He wanted to become a member of the Church, so Oliver took him to Seneca Lake and baptized him.

After his baptism, Brother Pratt was ordained an Elder. He then continued his journey to the home of his parents. He had a brother named Orson. He told him about the Prophet Joseph Smith, and the great work he was doing. Orson believed the good news, and his brother Parley baptized him.

After a brief visit with his folks, Parley returned to Fayette. There he had the pleasure of meeting the Prophet Joseph. A conference of the Church was held, which lasted three days. The Saints were greatly blessed, and a number of people were converted and baptized.

At that time the Lord called Oliver Cowdery,

Peter Whitmer, Jr., Ziba Peterson, and Parley P. Pratt to go on a mission to the Lamanites. Starting without delay, they journeyed towards Kirtland, Ohio, and preached the Gospel to the people in the villages along the way.

On nearing Kirtland, they came to the home of the young preacher, Sidney Rigdon. Brother Pratt told him all that had happened since they parted. Mr. Rigdon gave the brethren permission to preach in his chapel. He and his wife and a large number of his congregation were baptized. A branch of the Church was organized in that part of Ohio.

The missionaries then went to Kirtland, where they met with great success. Many people were converted, and a branch of the Church was organized.

After staying a short time in Kirtland, the brethren continued their journey. On coming to a tribe of Indians called the Wyandots, they stopped and preached the Gospel to them. Then they went on to Independence, a small town in Jackson county, Missouri. From there they passed into the State of Kansas, where they spent some time preaching to the Delaware Indians.

Since then the Gospel has been preached to thousands of the Lamanites. Hundreds of them have accepted it, and have become members of the Church. And thus some of the promises made to them in the Book of Mormon have been fulfilled.

THE FIRST BISHOP CHOSEN—GATHERING OF THE SAINTS TO OHIO.

In the month of December, 1830, two men came from Kirtland to see the Prophet. They found him at the home of his parents, near Fayette. One of these men was Sidney Rigdon, the young preacher who had joined the Church a short time before. The other was Edward Partridge.

After talking with the Prophet a short time, Mr. Partridge requested baptism. He was taken to Seneca Lake and there baptized by the Prophet Joseph. On the 4th day of February, 1831, Elder Partridge was appointed by revelation to be the first Bishop of the Church.

The Saints in the State of New York were being persecuted by their enemies. The Prophet Joseph visited them, and his presence gave them great joy. The Lord was watching over His people, and was preparing a place for them to move to.

On the 2nd day of February, 1831, the third conference of the Church was held at Fayette. It was a time of rejoicing for the Saints. They were promised many choice blessings from the Lord. They were told about a revelation which the Prophet Joseph had received a short time before. In that revelation the Saints were commanded to leave the State of New York and gather to Ohio. This they agreed to do as soon as possible.

Soon after the conference, Joseph, accompanied by his wife and several brethren, began the journey to Kirtland. They stopped at a number of places on the way and held meetings. Through the preaching of the Prophet and his brethren many people were added to the Church.

On arriving in Kirtland, the company stopped in front of a store. Joseph got out of the sleigh and went into the building. Going up to Mr. Whitney, a member of the firm, he offered him his hand, saying, "Newel K. Whitney! Thou art the man!"

Mr. Whitney looked quite surprised. He did not know the stranger. "You have the advantage of me," he said, as he shook Joseph's hand. "I could not call you by name as you have me."

Then Joseph said, "I am Joseph the Prophet. You have prayed me here, now what do you want of me?"

One evening, a short time before this, Mr. Whitney and his wife were praying to the Lord. While doing so they saw a bright cloud resting upon their house. Then they heard a voice from heaven, saying, "Prepare to receive the word of the Lord, for it is coming."

While Joseph was in the East, in a vision he saw them praying. That is why he knew Mr. Whitney.

Mr. Whitney took Joseph and his wife to his home. They stayed there several weeks, and were very kindly treated. The Whitneys afterwards joined the Church.

The following spring, all the branches of the Church in the State of New York removed to Ohio.

THE FOUNDATION OF ZION LAID.

In June, 1831, the fourth general conference was held in Kirtland. A little over a year before, the Church had been organized with six members. It now numbered two thousand.

The Prophet Joseph presided at the conference. It was a time of rejoicing for the Saints. The Lord poured out His Spirit upon them, and they saw and heard wonderful things. Joseph was filled with the spirit of prophecy. He said that John the Revelator was at that time with the Lost Tribes, preparing them for their return to the land of their fathers.

At this conference a number of missionaries were chosen, and sent out two by two to preach the Gospel. The Lord told the Prophet Joseph and Oliver Cowdery to go to the land of Missouri. He said that, if they proved faithful, He would reveal to them the place where the City of Zion, the New Jerusalem, would be built.

With this promise in mind, Joseph and a number of his brethren left Kirtland, on the 19th of June, 1831. They traveled by wagon and stage to Cincinnati, Ohio. From there they went by steamer to Louisville, Kentucky. At that place they had to wait three days for a vessel to take them to St. Louis. After resting a short time in St. Louis, Joseph and four of his companions started to walk across the entire State of Missouri. After traveling almost three hundred miles, they arrived in Independence.

Here they were joined by Oliver Cowdery and a number of other missionaries. The meeting was a joyful one, for Joseph had not seen his brethren since they started on their mission to the Lamanites.

Soon after the arrival of the Prophet and his party in Jackson county, Missouri, the Lord fulfilled His promise. He made known the place where the City of Zion would be established, which is where Independence is now built. He commanded the Saints to purchase the land in and around there and to gather to that place as soon as possible. He also revealed the spot where a great Temple would be built to His name.

A few days later the Saints of the Colesville branch arrived in Independence. They viewed with delight the land of Zion. It was, indeed, a beautiful place. Miles and miles of rich prairie land stretched before them. Wild flowers of almost every kind filled the air with their sweet perfume. There were large forests of choice timber. Buffalo, elk, deer, bear, wolves, beaver, and many smaller animals roamed round at pleasure. There was also a great variety of wild fowl, including turkeys, geese, swans and ducks.

On the 2nd day of August, 1831, the Prophet Joseph assisted the members of the Colesville Branch in laying the first log for a house, as a foundation of Zion. This took place in Kaw township, about 12 miles west of Independence. The log was carried by twelve men, in honor of the Twelve Tribes of Israel. Then the land of Zion was dedicated by Sidney Rigdon as a gathering place of the Saints.

The next day Joseph, accompanied by Sidney Rigdon, Edward Partridge, W. W. Phelps, Oliver Cowdery, Martin Harris, and Joseph Coe went to a spot a little west of Independence, and there the Prophet dedicated it as the site for the Temple of the Lord.

The first conference of the Church in the land of Zion was held on the 4th day of August, 1831, at the home of Brother Joshua Lewis. On the 19th of the same month the Propnet and ten of his brethren took leave of the Saints and started for Kirtland, arriving there August 27. They had been absent a little over two months, and had traveled two thousand miles.

A TERRIBLE NIGHT.

The Prophet Joseph and Sidney Rigdon were spending all their time in the work of the Lord. They were not getting any money for their labor. But they had friends who were kind to them and helped them.

One of these was a man named John Johnson, who lived at Hiram, Ohio. He took Joseph and Sidney to his home, and kept them and their families while they attended to certain work for the Church.

Emma Smith, the Prophet's wife, had adopted two little babies. They were twins, and were just eleven months old. They became very sick. Joseph and Emma watched over them with tender care. At night Joseph took charge of them while Emma slept.

Then she took her turn beside the sick-bed while her husband rested.

One night Mrs. Smith was almost worn out. Joseph told her to go to bed. He said he would sit up and take care of the child that was much worse than the other. As I write, I fancy I can see the Prophet watching beside the cot of the little sufferer, and praying for its recovery.

At last the baby fell asleep, and Joseph lay down upon his bed. In a little while he was asleep, too.

But what do you think had been going on outside? While Joseph was watching over the sick child, a mob of wicked men had gathered and were laying plans to kill him.

In the mob were a number of men who had left the Church. They had lost the Spirit of the Lord, and the spirit of the evil one had entered into them. They hated the Prophet and his work, and were trying to destroy them.

The mob came up to Mr. Johnson's place. They

burst into the house, and seizing Joseph, dragged him out into a meadow. Emma screamed, but she could not help her husband. Others of the mob laid hold of Sidney Rigdon and dragged him out, too.

Some of the wicked men wanted the Prophet to be killed. Others said, "No, we will not kill him, but we will tar and feather him."

Several of the mob held Joseph while others covered his body with tar. One of them tried to force the tar paddle into his mouth, but he kent his teeth tightly closed. Then they thrust a bottle of poison between his lips, but the bottle broke and the poison was spilled upon the ground.

When they had finished their awful work they ran away. Joseph was so weak that he could not stand. After a time he got strength, and made his way back to the house. There he found Brother Rigdon suffering terribly from the injuries he had received. Joseph spent the rest of the night getting the tar off his body.

The next day was Sunday. A meeting was held. The Prophet attended it and preached to the people. Several of the mob were in the meeting, but Joseph did not say anything about the mobbing. At the close of the service three persons were baptized. Soon after that Joseph and Sidney, with their families, moved from Hiram.

WHAT HAPPENED ON THE WAY TO KIRTLAND.

From Hiram, Ohio, the Prophet Joseph went to Missouri, to visit the Saints. Sidney Rigdon, Newel K. Whitney, Peter Whitmer and Jesse Gause went with him. They stayed there two weeks. During that time meetings were held, and the members of the Church had a delightful time.

Then Joseph decided to go to Kirtland, where his wife was. Newel K. Whitney and Sidney Rigdon accompanied him. There was no railroad in that part of the country. Most of the journey had to be made by stage.

One day a sad accident took place. The horses became frightened and ran away. Joseph jumped out of the stage. Newel K. Whitney also sprang out, but in doing so his foot caught in the wheel and his leg and foot were broken in several places.

Joseph helped Brother Whitney to a house owned by a man named Porter. They stayed there four weeks. During that time the Prophet administered often to his companion, which helped the sufferer very much.

The Porters were wicked people. One day they tried to kill the Prophet by putting poison in his food. Joseph had just finished his dinner. He felt a strange feeling come over him. He went outside and threw up much poisonous matter. That saved his life.

He returned to the house and told Newel what had happened. Brother Whitney laid his hands upon the head of the Prophet and prayed for him. His prayer was answered, and Joseph was healed.

They decided to leave the place at once. Newel wondered how they could get away. Joseph told him the Lord would provide means. The next morning a wagon drove up to the door. Joseph and Newel got into it and rode four miles to the river. There they found a ferryboat, on which they crossed to the other side. A carriage was waiting. They got into it and were driven to a boat which took them to Wellsville. From there they went by stage to Kirtland.

One day soon after Joseph had returned to Kirtland he was visited by three men. One of them was Brigham Young. This was the first time these men had met the Prophet. Brigham Young had been baptized into the Church about two months before.

The visiting brethren stayed in Kirtland four or five days. They saw and talked with the Prophet often.

One evening a meeting was held. Brigham Young arose and greatly surprised all present by speaking in a strange language. He had received from the Lord the gift of tongues. The Prophet Joseph was given the interpretation, and he told the people what Brother Young had said.

One day before Brigham Young left Kirtland Joseph pointed to him, saying: "That man will yet preside over this Church." You all know how that prophecy was fulfilled.

WORK OF A MISSOURI MOB.

The Church was organized on the 6th day of April, 1830. Three years later the Saints in Missouri met to celebrate its birthday. They were very happy. A glorious time was spent, and with joyful hearts the brethren and sisters returned to their homes. They had no thought at that time that in a little while their joy would be turned into sorrow.

Soon after this a mob of three hundred wicked men gathered at Independence. They hated the Saints, and had made up their minds to drive them from their homes and destroy the Church there.

But they did not succeed at that time. The leading brethren at Independence met together and prayed to the Lord to protect His people. Their prayer was answered. The mob became drunken, quarreled among themselves, and broke up without doing any harm to the Saints.

Three months passed, and then fresh trouble came to the Saints in Missouri. Five hundred men, enemies of the Church, met at Independence, on the 20th of July, 1833. They decided that from that time no Latter-day Saint should be permitted to settle in Jackson county; that the twelve hundred Saints who were there should leave, and that the Church paper —The Evening and Morning Star—should no longer be published.

A committee was appointed to call on the leading brethren and to tell them what had been decided at the meeting. You can imagine how the members of the Church felt when they heard the report. What was to be done? The brethren asked for ten days in which to think over the matter. The answer they received was, "Fifteen minutes are enough."

The committee returned and reported. The enemies of the Saints refused to wait. Headed by a red flag, they went to the home of Elder Wm. W. Phelps, where the Church paper was published, tore the printing office to the ground and carried away the type, press, and other things. Sister Phelps, with a sick babe in her arms, was turned out into the street. The mob then took Bishop Partridge and Elder Charles Allen to the courthouse, where they stripped them of their clothing and covered their bodies with tar and feathers.

The Lieutenant Governor of the State, Lilburn W. Boggs, was present and saw what took place. Instead of protecting the Saints, he made mock of them in their trouble, saying, "You now know what our Jackson boys can do, and you must leave the country."

Night came, and the wicked men, well pleased with what they had done, returned to their homes.

Three days later the mob met again. The Saints saw they were at the mercy of these wicked men. It would be a great trial to them to leave the houses and lands for which they had worked so hard. But by refusing to go they would bring upon themselves greater trouble—perhaps the loss of many lives.

They told the mob that one-half of their number would leave Missouri the 1st of the following January, and that the rest would follow the 1st of the next April. Their enemies agreed to this, and told the Saints they would not trouble them any more.

THE SAINTS DRIVEN FROM JACKSON COUNTY.

On hearing what the mob had done, Governor Dunklin advised the Saints to have their enemies arrested and tried by law. They decided to do so. They hired four lawyers at one thousand dollars to plead their cause in court.

When the enemies of the Saints heard this they became very angry. About fifty of them met and held a meeting. They were armed with guns and clubs. They decided to attack a little branch of the Church which was on the west bank of the Big Blue River, and destroy the homes of the Saints there.

When night came these wicked men went to the little settlement. All was peace and quiet. The Saints were asleep. Suddenly the doors of their homes were burst open, and the mob began its cruel work. The mothers and children were frightened almost to death. They ran screaming from their homes and hid themselves among the bushes. The husbands and fathers tried to escape, but failed. They were caught by the mob, and were badly beaten with clubs and other weapons.

When their enemies had left, the women and children crept from their hiding places. They made their way back towards their humble homes, but found some of them in ruins. These are some of the things which the Saints in those days suffered because they would not deny the truth.

Night after night the work of destruction was carried on. The mob broke into the store owned by Gilbert and Whitney, threw some of the goods into the street, and carried much away.

A few days later the mob decided to make another attack upon the Saints at Independence. A number of the brethren armed themselves with guns. They felt that it was right for them to protect themselves, their wives and children. There were sixty wicked men in the mob. When they came to the place where the Saints were they fired upon them, wounding several. Two of the brethren, Andrew Barber and Philo Dibble, were seriously wounded. Brother Dibble recovered, but Brother Barber died the next day. He laid down his life for his friends.

The mob was stopped in its deadly work by the guns of the Saints. When the mob opened fire, some of the brethren who had guns used them. Two of their enemies fell dead. The rest became frightened and ran away, leaving their horses and dead companions.

A report of the battle soon spread over the country. Then followed a time of great excitement. Wicked falsehoods were told about the Saints. It was said they were going to drive the rest of the people out of the country. Instead of that it was the Saints who were about to be driven.

One of the bitterest enemies of the Saints was Lieutenant-Governor Boggs. What do you think he did at this time? He organized a company of the state militia, which many of the mob joined, and placed Colonel Pitcher, as wicked a man as himself, in charge.

Pitcher ordered the Saints to deliver up their guns, and to leave the country at once. He deceived them ' by telling them that their enemies would have to give up their weapons also. He also told the Saints he would give them protection.

The members of the Church had been taught to obey the laws of the land, and to be subject to those in authority. They, therefore, turned over their weapons.

Then a mob of human fiends attacked their homes. They drove out helpless women and children, and threatened to take their lives if they did not leave the country. Frightened almost to death, the poor Saints fled in all directions. Some of them stayed

7

all night on the open prairie, while others sought protection along the banks of the Missouri River.

When the Prophet heard what had taken place, he burst into tears. "Oh, my brethren, my brethren," he sobbed, "would that I had been with you to share your fate."

ZION'S CAMP.

The Saints who were driven from Jackson county settled in Clay, Van Buren and Lafayette counties. They were very kindly treated by the citizens of Clay county.

The Prophet Joseph prayed often to the Lord for them. He was told in a revelation to organize a company to assist them, and to try to get their homes restored to them. He organized the company and gave it the name Zion's Camp.

The company left Kirtland on the 5th of May, 1834. It was led by the Prophet Joseph. There were about one hundred and fifty men in the party. They had twenty wagons filled with food and clothing for their poor brethren and sisters in Missouri. Nearly all the brethren had to walk. Sometimes they traveled forty miles in a day. They rested Sundays and held meetings.

Each night at the sound of a trumpet the men went to their tents. They knelt down and thanked the Lord for His blessings. They also prayed for the dear ones they had left behind. In the morning when the trumpet sounded, the men of the camp knelt upon the ground and asked the Lord to take care of them during the day.

One evening, when some of the brethren were putting up the Prophet's tent, they saw three rattlesnakes. They were about to kill them when Joseph stopped them. "Men must become harmless themselves," he said, "before they can expect the brute creation to be so."

A few days later one of the company, Solomon Humphrey, lay down on the prairie to rest. While he slept, a large rattlesnake coiled itself up near his head. When Brother Humphrey awoke and saw the serpent, he said to some of the brethren who would have killed it, "No, I will protect him, for he and I have had a good nap together." The rattlesnake's life was spared.

The journey to Missouri was a very trying one. At times the men had to wade through rivers and struggle through swamps. With bruised and bleeding feet they traveled over hills and sandy plains. Because of these trials some of them began to murmur. Joseph spoke kindly to them. He pleaded with them to stop finding fault, and to humble themselves before the Lord. He said the Lord had revealed to him that if they did not do so, a scourge would come upon the camp.

After traveling a little over a month, Joseph and his brethren arrived at Salt River, in the State of Missouri. Here they were joined by another party which Hyrum Smith and Lyman Wight had gathered in the State of Michigan and other places. There were now two hundred and five men and twenty-five wagons in Zion's Camp.

After resting several days at Salt River, the Camp proceeded on its journey. On hearing of the coming of Joseph and his brethren, a mob of wicked men started to raise an army to attack them. The leaders of the mob were Samuel C. Owens and James Campbell. As Campbell placed his pistols in his belt he said he would fix Joe Smith and his army before two days were past.

He did not live to carry out his threat. That night, as twelve of the mob were trying to cross the Missouri River, the boat sank and seven men were drowned. Campbell was one of them. In seeking the lives of others, he lost his own.

HOW THE LORD PROTECTED HIS PEOPLE.

The members of Zion's Camp were in great danger. They were surrounded by wicked men who had made up their minds to murder them. And they would, no doubt, have done so, if the Lord had not prevented them.

On the night of June 19, 1834, Joseph and his party passed safely through the town of Richmond. They camped between two branches of Fishing River. They were getting ready to lie down to rest when five rough men, with loaded guns, appeared before them. "You shall not live to see morning," they said. "Sixty men are coming from Richmond, and seventy more from Clay county, to utterly destroy you."

How easy it is for the Lord to overthrow the plans

of wicked men. You remember reading in the Bible how He saved the children of Israel from the Egyptians. Well, in much the same way He saved the members of Zion's Camp.

That night a terrible storm arose. The lightning flashed, the thunder rolled, and rain came down in torrents. Some of the mob said afterwards that Little Fishing River rose thirty feet in thirty minutes. The awful storm filled the enemies of the Saints with fear. They fled in all directions, trying to find shelter. One of their number was struck by lightning and killed.

Where were the members of Zion's Camp all this time? They were safe and dry in a schoolhouse. How grateful they all felt! From the heart of each one there went up a prayer of thanksgiving to the Lord for His protecting care.

Two days later, three leading men of Ray county came to see the Prophet. He received them kindly. One of them said, "We see that there is an Almighty

power that protects this people." He told Joseph that he was leading an armed mob against him and his party when the storm burst upon them and drove them back.

The Prophet told them the mission of Zion's Camp. He said they were carrying food and clothing to their poor brethren and sisters who had been driven from their homes in Independence. They had no thought of doing harm to anyone.

Before Joseph had finished speaking the three men were shedding tears. They offered the Prophet their hands, and told him they would do all in their power to stop the cruel work of the enemies of the Saints.

Soon after this, Zion's Camp was disbanded. Taking a few faithful brethren with him, Joseph went to Independence. He felt very sorrowful as he looked upon the lands from which his people had been driven. They were then in the hands of their enemies. But he was made glad on remembering what the

Lord had told him in a revelation a short time before—that the day would come when Zion would be redeemed, and the Saints would again possess the land.

After visiting several days among the members of the Church, Joseph returned to Kirtland.

THE BOOK OF ABRAHAM.

For three years the Church had peace. The Saints made good use of the time. The Lord had commanded them to build a Temple in Kirtland. There were only thirty families of Saints in that place. They were very poor, and they had to make great sacrifices in order to build the Temple. The Prophet Joseph worked in the stone quarry, and his brother Hyrum also labored faithfully on the sacred building.

The Lord had revealed to the Prophet Joseph that Twelve Apostles should be called to preach the Gospel, and to assist the First Presidency in presiding over the Church. The time had now come for these men to be chosen. They were selected from the members of Zion's Camp. Their names were: Thomas B. Marsh, David W. Patten, Brigham

Young, Heber C. Kimball, William Smith, Orson Pratt, Orson Hyde, William E. McLellin, Parley P. Pratt, Luke Johnson, John F. Boynton and Lyman E. Johnson.

A few days later the First Quorum of Seventy was organized. Soon after their ordination the Apostles were called to go on missions. They traveled like the early Apostles—without purse or scrip. They were blessed of the Lord. Kind friends took care of them, and through their preaching many were brought into the Church.

One day a French traveler, Mr. Michael H. Chandler, came to Kirtland to see the Prophet. He had with him four mummies and some rolls of papyrus. These had been found in Thebes, Egypt, by Mr. Chandler's uncle.

Mr. Chandler had shown the mummies and papyrus to learned men in Philadelphia. They were able to translate only a few of the characters which were upon the parchment. On hearing of Joseph Smith, and that he was able to translate strange writings, Mr. Chandler brought the mummies and manuscript to him.

Joseph examined the characters upon the parchment, and to his surprise and delight found they had been written by Abraham. By the power of God he translated some of the characters, and Mr. Chandler said it was much better than the learned men of Philadelphia had done.

Some friends of the Prophet bought the mummies and parchment from Mr. Chandler. Joseph translated the writing which was upon the parchment. Then it was printed in a book. You can find it in "The Pearl of Great Price." It is called "The Book of Abraham."

REMARKABLE VISIONS IN KIRTLAND TEMPLE.

For three years the Saints worked faithfully on the Kirtland Temple. At the end of that time the sacred building was finished and dedicated. The dedication took place on the 27th of March, 1836.

One day, about two months before the dedication, the Prophet Joseph, his two counselors, Sidney Rigdon and Frederick G. Williams and the Prophet's father went to the Temple. There Father Smith was anointed as the Patriarch of the Church. He anointed and blessed Joseph and his counselors. Just then a wonderful thing took place. The heavens were opened and a glorious vision was given to the Prophet. He saw the celestial kingdom, and beheld its glory. He saw a beautiful throne, on which were seated the Father and the Son. He also saw fathers Adam and Abraham, and was told things which you will learn as you grow older.

Joseph's father and the other brethren were also greatly blessed of the Lord. Some of them beheld the Savior, and others saw holy angels. They rejoiced and praised the Lord for the glorious things they had seen and heard.

The evening of the dedication Joseph met with the quorums of the Priesthood in the Temple. While Brother George A. Smith was speaking, a noise was heard like the rushing of a strong wind. The whole congregation arose at once. Some spoke in tongues, others prophesied and others saw heavenly visions. The Temple was filled with angels. People outside heard the strange sound, and came running to the Temple. They beheld a bright light, like a pillar of fire, resting above the sacred building.

On Sunday, the 3rd of April, 1836, while the Prophet Joseph and Oliver Cowdery were praying in

the Temple a remarkable vision was given to them.
They saw the Lord standing upon the breastwork of
the pulpit. His eyes were as a flame of fire. His
hair was white as pure snow, and His face was
brighter than the sun. He spoke to Joseph and
Oliver, saying:

"I am the first and the last; I am he who liveth, I
am he who was slain, I am your advocate with the
Father;

"Behold, your sins are forgiven you, you are clean
before me, therefore lift up your heads and rejoice.

"Let the hearts of your brethren rejoice, and let
the hearts of all my people rejoice, who have with
their might built this house to my name.

"For behold, I have accepted this house, and my
name shall be here, and I will manifest myself to my
people in mercy in this house;

"Yea, I will appear unto my servants, and speak
unto them with mine own voice, if my people will

keep my commandments, and do not pollute this holy house.

"Yea, the hearts of thousands and tens of thousands shall greatly rejoice in consequence of the blessings which shall be poured out, and the endowment with which my servants have been endowed in this house;

"And the fame of this house shall spread to foreign lands, and this is the beginning of the blessing which shall be poured out upon the heads of my people. Even so. Amen."

The word of the Lord has been fulfilled. The fame of the Kirtland Temple has spread into foreign lands, and people of many nations have heard of the wonderful visions and revelations which were given in that holy place.

After the vision of the Savior, Moses, Elias and Elijah appeared to Joseph and Oliver. Moses gave them authority to gather the people of the Lord from the nations of the earth, and Elijah revealed to them

8

the work for the dead. This work is now being done in the Temples, and the dead as well as the living are receiving the blessings of the Gospel.

THE BRITISH MISSION OPENED.

No greater work was ever done by mortal man than by the Prophet Joseph Smith. Tens of thousands of people in this land praise his name for the blessings they have received through him. As you know, it was through Joseph the Gospel was restored. The Gospel was taken to the lands in which the British people lived. They received it, and it has brought to them peace, joy and happiness such as they never had before.

That is not all. Many of them were found in the depths of poverty. But the Lord opened the way for them to come to Zion, where they have been blessed with houses and lands, orchards and vineyards, and now live surrounded with peace and plenty.

In the year 1837 the Lord revealed to the Prophet

Joseph that missionaries should be sent to Great Britain. Apostle Heber C. Kimball was chosen to take charge of this work. A better selection could not have been made. Elder Kimball was a man of strong faith. He loved the Gospel. It had brought such joy to his soul that he was willing to make any sacrifice to carry the glad tidings to others.

Apostle Orson Hyde and Elders Willard Richards and Joseph Fielding were called to go with Brother Kimball. On reaching New York they were joined by three brethren from Canada. The company sailed from the United States on the 1st of July, 1837, on the ship Garrick, and on the 20th of the same month arrived in Liverpool, England.

The missionaries decided to go to Preston, a town about thirty miles from Liverpool. Elder Fielding had a brother, a minister, living at that place. On getting out of the coach at Preston, one of the first things the brethren saw was a large flag, on which were the words, "Truth will prevail." Just three simple words, but they filled the hearts of the servants of the Lord with hope and courage.

The Sunday morning after the arrival of the missionaries in Preston, the Reverend Mr. Fielding told the members of his church assembled in meeting that some ministers from America would preach in his chapel that afternoon. You can imagine how glad the brethren felt. Elders Kimball and Hyde addressed the meeting in the afternoon. They told the people about the Prophet Joseph Smith, and some of the wonderful things which the Lord had revealed to him.

Another meeting was held in the evening, and one on the following Wednesday night. Some of the members of Mr. Fielding's church were beginning to believe the teachings of the Elders. That displeased the minister, and he told the missionaries he would not allow them to preach in his chapel any more. They met, however, in the homes of some of the people, and at the end of a week nine persons were baptized into the Church.

One morning, soon after that, the missionaries were attacked by evil spirits. Their room was filled with them. Brother Kimball was sorely afflicted. The brethren prayed to the Lord to deliver them. He rebuked the evil spirits, and the brethren had peace.

The Lord blessed the labors of His faithful servants, so that in five months one thousand people were converted and made members of the true Church. This was the beginning of the great latter-day work in England.

THE HAUN'S MILL MASSACRE.

While a glorious work was being done for the Church in England, it was having a very hard time at home. It had not only foes without but foes within. A number of its leading men did things that were wrong, and they were cut off from membership in the Church. Some of them turned against the work of the Lord and tried to destroy it .

It was a terrible time for the Saints in Missouri. Each day brought them fresh trouble. Their enemies had made up their minds to either destroy them or drive them out of the state.

One day a mob of wicked men entered the little town of De Witt, in Carroll county, where a number of the Saints resided. They had guns and cannon, and at once opened fire on the town. The Saints.

defended themselves as well as they could. They had to stay in their homes for two days.

Their enemies decided to starve them out. They set fire to some of the homes, and killed and roasted a number of cattle. When the Saints saw they could not hold out any longer they agreed to leave the place. They were promised pay for their homes and other property, but they did not receive anything. The Saints fled to Far West. But before reaching that place some of their number died. One poor mother, with a baby a day old, could not stand the journey. She died, and had to be buried without a coffin.

Soon after this a wicked mob, led by a scoundrel named Bogart, attacked a camp of the Saints on Crooked River. They took three of the brethren prisoners, and said they would put them to death before nightfall.

Word was sent at once to Far West. Apostle David W. Patten quickly gathered fifty men and started with them for the scene of the capture. They came in sight of Bogart's camp at daybreak. Bogart's men were hidden behind trees, and as the brethren drew near they opened fire on them. In the battle which followed Apostle Patten lost his life. As he was dying that night, surrounded by the Prophet Joseph and a number of friends, he turned to his wife and said, "Whatever else you do, do not deny the faith."

Then the whole State of Missouri was aroused. Lieutenant-Governor Boggs ordered out two thousand men, and told them to either kill the "Mormons" or drive them out of the state. They began at once to carry out his instructions. Two hundred and forty of them went to a settlement of the Saints at Haun's Mill, in Caldwell county, and without a moment's warning began to fire upon men, women and children.

The poor Saints pleaded for mercy, but the wretches paid no heed to their cries. In a little while they had killed seventeen members of the Church. There was an old well near by, and the bodies of the murdered Saints were thrown into it.

These good Latter-day Saints laid down their lives for the truth's sake, and great shall be their reward in heaven. But woe to those who so foully murdered them. Better for them if they had never been born.

THE PROPHET JOSEPH IN RICHMOND JAIL.

Soon after the terrible massacre at Haun's Mill, a large army of mob militia gathered at Richmond. From here they marched to within a short distance of Far West, where they camped. One morning, a few days later, men carrying a white flag were seen approaching the City of Far West. They were members of the militia. The white flag was a sign of peace.

Colonel Hinkle went out to meet the men. He went back with them to their camp, and there he entered into an agreement with the enemies of the Saints to deliver the Prophet Joseph and a number of the leading brethren into their hands. The name of this traitor may well be linked with that of Judas Iscariot.

He returned to Far West and told the Prophet that the officers in charge of the militia desired him and other leading men to come to their camp that night. They wished, he said, to have the difficulties settled. Joseph asked Hinkle for the names of the other brethren, and he said they were Sidney Rigdon, Parley P. Pratt, Lyman Wight, and George W. Robinson. Hinkle assured the Prophet that no harm would come to him or his brethren.

Hinkle accompanied Joseph and his brethren to the camp of the militia, and there the true character of the traitor was revealed. Addressing General Lucas he said, "These are the prisoners I agreed to deliver up." The whole camp yelled with delight, and General Lucas brandished his sword as if he had gained a great victory.

The Prophet and his companions were immediately placed in charge of strong guards. They had to lie upon the wet ground. They were kept awake all night with the mockings, curses and threats of the vile wretches in charge of them. The next morning Hyrum Smith and Amasa M. Lyman were dragged from their families in Far West, and brought into the camp.

It was decided to send the prisoners to Independence. The Saints at Far West were told by the mob that they need never expect to see their leaders again, for their doom was sealed. However, while Joseph and his companions were camped at night on Crooked River the word of the Lord came to the Prophet assuring him that their lives would be spared.

The next morning Joseph spoke to his fellow-prisoners in a low, cheerful tone, saying: "Be of good cheer, my brethren, the word of the Lord came to me last night that our lives should be given us, and that whatever else we might have to suffer during this captivity, not one of us should die."

The prisoners were taken to Independence. A few days later General Clark gave orders for them to be taken to Richmond and placed in jail there. On the way the guards got drunk. It would have been easy for Joseph and his brethren to have made their escape. They knew, however, that they had not broken any law. If they were to run away people would say they were guilty. All they wanted was a fair trial. They knew they could prove their innocence. The Prophet and his companions took charge of the guards' guns and horses, and returned them to the guards when the latter became sober.

On arriving in Richmond the brethren were taken to the jail, and there they were bound with chains and placed in charge of as vile wretches as ever lived. They had to lie upon the bare floor, without any covering.

The Prophet and his friends suffered terribly, not only in body but also in spirit. Night after night they had to listen to the vulgar songs and stories, the curses and laughter of those who kept guard over them.

One night the wretches were telling with great glee

The Prophet Rebuking the Guards.

of the way in which they had treated some of the Saints. They boasted of the awful crimes they had committed upon mothers and daughters, and that they had even killed little children.

Suddenly the Prophet sprang to his feet, and in a voice that almost shook the prison he rebuked the inhuman monsters. "Silence!" said he, "ye fiends of the infernal pit! In the name of Jesus Christ I rebuke you and command you to be still; I will not live another minute and hear such language. Cease such talk, or you or I die this instant!"

"He ceased speaking. He stood erect in terrible majesty. Chained, and without a weapon, calm, unruffled and dignified as an angel, he looked down upon the quailing guards, whose knees smote together, and who, shrinking into a corner, or crouching at his feet, begged his pardon, and remained quiet until change of guards."

FROM MISSOURI TO ILLINOIS—A DAY OF MIRACULOUS HEALINGS.

I have not told you a hundredth part of the sufferings of the Saints in Missouri. They were not only robbed of their homes, their lands, cattle, etc., but between three and four hundred of them—men, women and children—were murdered in cold blood. Sister Amanda Smith, whose husband and little son were murdered at Haun's Mill, says:

"The mob told us we must leave the state forthwith or be killed. It was cold weather, and they had our teams and clothes, our men all dead or wounded. I told them they might kill me and my children and welcome. They sent word to us from time to time, saying that if we did not leave the state they would come and kill us. We had little prayer meetings. They said if we did not stop them they would kill every man, woman and child. We had spelling schools for our little children. They said if we did not stop these they would kill every man, woman and child. We (the women) had to do our own milking, cut our own wood; no man to help us. I started on the 1st of February for Illinois, without money; mobs on the way; drove our own teams; slept out of doors. I had five small children; we suffered hunger, fatigue and cold."

The people of Illinois had heard of the terrible persecutions of the Saints in Missouri. They felt sorry for them, and were willing to help them. So, on being driven from Missouri, the Saints took up their abode in Illinois. There, on the banks of the Mississippi River, they founded the beautiful little city of Nauvoo.

After being in prisons for almost six months, Joseph and his brethren regained their liberty and joined the Saints in Illinois. There was much joy among the members of the Church when their beloved Prophet appeared in their midst again. He found his family very poor. Their home was a little log cabin, but even for it they were thankful .

Nauvoo was a beautiful place for a city. The Mississippi swept around it in a half circle, giving the place three fronts upon the noble river. But it proved to be an unhealthful place, for soon after the Saints had settled there many of them suffered with malarial fever.

The Prophet himself was afflicted and confined to his bed; but through the power of the Lord he overcame the disease and went forth and began to administer to many who were ill. He walked along the bank of the river, healing all the sick who lay in his path. Going to the tent of Brother Henry G. Sherwood, who was almost at the point of death, he commanded him in the name of the Lord Jesus Christ to arise and be made well. Brother Sherwood was

Nauvoo—The Beautiful.

healed immediately, and arose and walked out of the tent. Joseph, with Elder Heber C. Kimball and others, then crossed the river to Montrose. There they found several of the Apostles very ill. They were also healed, and straightway arose and went with the Prophet to administer to other sick persons.

They first called at the home of Brother Elijah Fordham, who it was expected every minute would die. Joseph walked up to the dying man, and took hold of his right hand and spoke to him; but Brother Fordham was unable to speak; his eyes were set in his head like glass, and he seemed entirely unconscious of all around him. Joseph held his hand and looked into his eyes in silence for a short time. A change in Brother Fordham was soon noticed by all present. His sight returned, and upon Joseph asking him if he knew him, he, in a low whisper, answered, "Yes." Joseph asked him if he had faith to be healed. He answered, "I fear it is too late; if you had come sooner, I think I could have been healed." The Prophet said, "Do you not believe in Jesus Christ?" He answered in a feeble voice, "I do." Joseph then stood erect still holding his hand in silence several moments. Then he spoke in a loud voice, saying, "Brother Fordham, I command you in the name of Jesus Christ to arise from this bed and be made whole." His voice was like the voice of God, and not of man. It seemed as though the house shook to its very foundation. Brother Fordham arose from his bed and was healed that moment. He put on his clothes, and after eating a bowl of bread and milk, followed the Prophet into the street.

These things strengthened greatly the faith of the Saints, who gave thanks and praise to the Lord for the power which He had given to His servants.

The Healing of Ethel Fanshawe

THE PROPHET'S VISIT TO WASHINGTON.

Joseph now decided to go to Washington, and make a full report to the President of the United States and Congress of the wrongs which his people had suffered in Missouri. The Saints at that time were very poor, for they had been robbed of almost all their property. The Prophet hoped to be able to get them help. He felt that the State of Missouri should be made pay the Saints for the great loss they had suffered.

In the month of October, 1839, in company with Sidney Rigdon and Judge Elias Higbee, Joseph started for the national capital. They traveled by stage. There were in the coach some women and children, also two or three members of Congress.

One day while they were traveling through the

mountains the driver stopped at a house to get some liquor. While he was gone, the horses became frightened and started to run at full speed down a steep hill. The women screamed, and one lady, fearing she would be killed, was about to throw her baby out of the window when the Prophet got hold of her and kept her from doing so.

Of all the passengers, he was the least excited. When he had calmed the women, he opened the door and climbed up into the driver's seat. Then he got hold of the reins, and in a little while brought the horses under control and stopped them. They had run about three miles.

The passengers gave much praise and thanks to the young man for his brave act. Had it not been for his heroic work perhaps some of them would have lost their lives. The gentlemen from Washington said they would call the attention of Congress to the noble deed. They asked the Prophet his name. He told them he was Joseph Smith. On hearing that,

The Prophet Joseph Stopping the Runaway.

they looked at each other in surprise and said no more about the matter.

On the way, Sidney Rigdon took sick, and had to be left at Philadelphia. Soon after their arrival in Washington, the Prophet Joseph and Judge Higbee called upon President Van Buren and gave him their letters of introduction. When he had learned their errand, a frown came over his face, and he said sharply, "I can do nothing for you. If I do anything I shall come in contact with the whole State of Missouri."

Then Joseph told him of the terrible wrongs which had been done to the Saints in Missouri. As he related them, the feelings of the President seemed to change, and he said he would think the matter over.

When the Prophet and his companion called on the President again they were surprised to find that he had no desire to help the poor people who had been so cruelly wronged. "Your cause is just," he said; "but I can do nothing for you. If I take up for you, I shall lose the vote of Missouri."

A committee had been appointed by Congress to consider the matter, but the members of it, like the President, were afraid to do anything in behalf of the despised "Mormons."

But Joseph's mission to Washington was not an entire failure. He preached several public sermons, and made many warm friends, who afterwards wrote and spoke well of him.

REMARKABLE PROPHECIES AND THEIR FULFILLMENT

One day a number of Indians came to Nauvoo to see the Prophet. Some of them had read the Book of Mormon, and they wanted to meet the man who had sent them the wonderful history.

Joseph told them about their forefathers, who had come across the great waters to this land. He told the Indians of the many ways in which the Lord had blessed their fathers. But because they would not do as the Lord told them, but quarreled and fought among themselves, He was angry with them and caused a dark skin to come upon many of them.

The Prophet told the Indians that if they would do right, and live in peace, the Lord would bless them and they would be happy. When he had finished speaking one of the chiefs said: "I believe you are a great and good man. I look rough, but I am also a son of the Great Spirit. I have heard your voice; and we intend to quit fighting, and follow the good advice you have given us."

Nauvoo grew very fast. In less than two years there were thousands of Saints living there in good homes. A university was planned, and later the city was crowned with a beautiful Temple.

The Prophet felt, however, that his people would not remain there long. One day he crossed the river to Montrose. Standing in the shade of a building there he uttered a remarkable prophecy. He said the Saints would continue to suffer much affliction, and would be driven to the Rocky Mountains. Many would leave the Church, others would be put to death or lose their lives through disease, and because of the trials that would come to them; but some of those present would live to go and help make settlements and build cites and see the Saints

Joseph Preaching to the Indians.

become a mighty people in the midst of the Rocky Mountains. That was a wonderful prophecy. It has been fulfilled to the very letter.

One night the Prophet Joseph, Wilford Woodruff and Willard Richards were out walking together, and talking about the great latter-day work. Suddenly a strange light appeared in the heavens. It was in the shape of a sword. As they stood looking at it, Joseph told them that it was a sign of a terrible war which would take place in this country.

Some years before this he prophesied about this great war. He said it would be brought about by the Southern States rebelling against the Northern States; that the Southern States would call on Great Britain for help; that the war would begin in South Carolina, and that it would end in the death of many men.

About twenty-eight years later this prophecy began to be fulfilled. The Southern States rebelled against the Northern States, which brought about the great Civil War. The war commenced where the Prophet said it would, in South Carolina, and it ended in the death of over one million men.

Before closing this chapter I wish to tell you about another prophecy which Joseph gave in the month of May, 1843. He was dining at Carthage, Illinois, with Judge Stephen A. Douglas and others. After dinner, Judge Douglas asked the Prophet to give him an account of the persecutions of the Saints in Missouri. Joseph did so, talking for almost three hours.

At that time the judge seemed to be very friendly towards the Prophet. When Joseph had told him all that the Saints had passed through, he looked straight into Mr. Douglas' face and said: "Judge, you will aspire to the Presidency of the United States; and if you ever turn your hand against me or the Latter-day Saints, you will feel the weight of the hand of the Almighty upon you;

and you will live to see and know that I have testified the truth to you; for the conversation of this day will stick to you through life."

Seventeen years afterwards Mr. Douglas was named for President of the United States. It was firmly believed that he would be elected, for he was looked upon as a great man. But, in order to make friends of those who were opposed to the Saints, he turned against the Latter-day Saints, and said many things about them which were false and wicked.

Well, the day of the election came, and Judge Douglas was defeated; he was voted down in every State in the Union except one. It was at that time that Abraham Lincoln was made President.

In less than a year Judge Douglas died at his home in Chicago, a disappointed and almost broken-hearted man.

A COLD-BLOODED MURDER.

On the 6th day of April, 1844, a special conference of the Church was held in Nauvoo. There were twenty thousand people present. The Prophet seemed to be filled with the Spirit of the Lord. He preached for three and a half hours, and during all that time the people sat in silence, drinking in the glorious truths that fell from his lips. That sermon will never be forgotten. People often talk about it now.

At that time a number of men were cut off from the Church. Their names were William Law, Wilson Law, Chauncy L. Higbee, Francis M. Higbee, and Robert D. Foster. They had been found guitly of wicked things. They had even gone so far as to lay plans to kill the Prophet.

These vile traitors went to Carthage, Illinois, and made false and wicked charges against the Prophet Joseph.   On hearing that an order had been issued for his arrest, Joseph went to Carthage and placed himself in charge of an officer of the court. All he wanted was a fair trial, and that it be held at once.   The other side, however, wanted the case held back for a time.   It was decided to do this. Joseph was given in charge of the sheriff; but that officer allowed him to return with his compaions to Nauvoo.   Joseph learned later that it was the intention of his enemies to kill him that night in Carthage.

On the night of the 22nd of June, 1844, Joseph and his brother, Hyrum left Nauvoo.   They had decided to go to the Rocky Mountains, to escape from their enemies, and to choose a place of safety and rest for the Saints.   Tears streamed down the Prophet's cheeks as he bade good-by to his loved ones.

Some time after Joseph and Hyrum had left, Emma Smith, the Prophet's wife, and others sent messengers after them, asking them to come back, as they were being spoken of as cowards. They turned at once and started back towards Nauvoo. "Hyrum," said Joseph, "we are going back to be murdered." To this Hyrum replied, "If we live or die we will be reconciled to our fate."

Next morning Joseph, with seventeen others, started for Carthage. On the way Joseph said to his companions, "I am going like a lamb to the slaughters, but I am calm as a summer's morning. I have a conscience void of offense toward God and toward all men. If they take my life I shall die an innocent man, and my blood shall cry from the ground for vengeance, and it shall yet be said of me, 'He was murdered in cold blood'."

On the 27th of June, 1844, the Prophet Joseph, his brother, Hyrum, Apostles John Taylor and Willard Richards were sitting as prisoners in

Hyrum Smith, the Patriarch.

Carthage jail. They were very sad, for they felt that something awful was going to happen. Joseph asked Brother Taylor to sing a hymn, which he did.

A little later the brethren saw a number of men with painted faces running around the jail. They had guns in their hands. They rushed up the stairway, burst open the door and began firing upon the prisoners. The beloved Hyrum was the first to fall. He received three bullets, and sank to the floor, saying, "I am a dead man." Joseph sprang to the window. As he stood for a second looking out, two bullets from behind and one from the mob in front pierced his body, and he fell to the ground exclaiming, "My Lord! my God!" Elder Taylor received five bullet wounds, but, strange to tell, they did not prove fatal. Elder Richards was left unharmed.

Thus ended the mortal lives of two of the noblest and best men the world has ever seen. Save Jesus of Nazareth, no greater Prophet ever lived than Joseph Smith.

"Praise to his memory, he died as a martyr,

Honored and blessed be his ever great name;

Long shall his blood which was shed by assassins

Stain Illinois, while the earth lauds his fame."